Easy Knitted Accessories

COMPILED BY **Amy Palmer**

INTERWEAVE.
interweave.com

*The projects in this collection were
originally published in other Interweave
publications, including* Interweave Crochet, Interweave Knits, Knitscene, *and*
Piecework *magazines and* CrochetMe
*eBooks. Some have been altered to
update information and/or conform to
space limitations.*

Interweave Press LLC,
a division of F+W Media Inc
201 East Fourth Street
Loveland, CO 80537
interweave.com

Printed in the United States
by Versa Press

Table of Contents

Circular KNITTING
a.k.a. KNITTING IN THE ROUND

Being able to knit with circular needles to create a tubular fabric has one big advantage—no seams. Plus, if you're knitting stockinette, you never have to purl!

To knit in the round, you'll need an array of sizes in double-pointed (sets of four or five) and circular needles. Circular needles are available in different lengths, the most common being 16" (40.5 cm), 24" (61 cm), and 29" (73.5 cm). The circular needle used must be shorter than the circumference of the garment. You can compact the stitches on the needle, but you can't stretch out work that is too narrow. The shortest circular needle available is 9" (23 cm), so any garment with a narrower circumference must be worked on double-pointed needles that can accommodate as

little as one stitch per needle. Socks or gloves can be worked on a 9" (23 cm) circular needle but are more easily worked on double-pointed needles. A 16" (40.5 cm) needle is a good length for a hat with a 21" (53.5 cm) circumference, but you'll need to switch to double-pointed needles as you begin decreasing to shape the crown. The pattern will designate what size and length circular needle is recommended or whether double-pointed needles are better. The abbreviation for double-pointed needles is dpn and many knitters refer to them by the abbreviation.

Pattern directions for circular knitting call the rows "rounds." The major difference between working in rounds and working back and forth in rows is that when you're working in rounds, you don't turn the work. Because the right side of the work is always facing you, you don't need to change knit stitches to purl stitches on the wrong side of the work. For this reason, if you are working in rounds in stockinette stitch, every stitch will be a knit stitch. If you are working rounds in ribbing, simply work each stitch as it appears to maintain the continuity of the rib.

The trickiest part of circular knitting is getting started. To knit in the round on circular needles, cast on the recommended number of stitches, just as you would if working on straight needles. Make sure all the cast-on stitches are hanging below the needle and are not twisted around the needle. (This is the most common error—stitches get twisted in the process of casting on and the

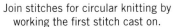

Join stitches for circular knitting by working the first stitch cast on.

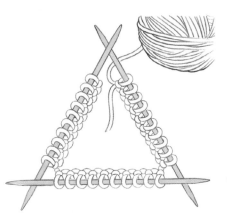

FIGURE 1. Divide the stitches among three (or four) double-pointed needles.

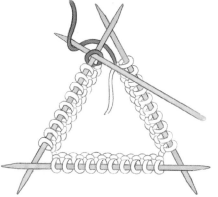

FIGURE 2. Join for circular knitting by working the first cast-on stitch.

Illustrations: Sara Boore

only alternative is to rip out and cast on again.) Now hold one needle tip in each hand with the end of the needle connected to the working yarn in your right hand. Depending on the stitch pattern, knit or purl into the first stitch on the left-hand needle—this was the first cast-on stitch. Again, be careful not to twist stitches. After this first connecting stitch is made, work the rest of the round according to pattern. You may want to place a stitch marker on the needle to help you keep track of the first stitch of the round. You'll slip this marker as you work each round.

If you're using double-pointed needles, after casting the stitches onto one needle, divide the total number of stitches evenly between three or four needles (needles usually come in sets of four or five, but you need one to knit with) by sliding stitches over from either end **(figure 1)**.

Once you have the stitches on your needles, arrange them in a triangle (or four needles in a square) so that the cast-on edge faces the inside. Now you're ready to join your work. With the spare needle, begin to knit with the yarn from the right-hand needle, pulling the first stitch firmly to eliminate a gap **(figure 2)**. After the first stitch, use a marker to mark the beginning of each new round. Work to the end of the first needle and use that needle as a spare to work stitches from the next needle. Continue in this manner around. 🖋

The Jogless Jog

Knitting color stripes in the round can result in jogs at the "seam" line where each new round begins. This occurs because the first stitch in the row above a color change is actually the last stitch of the previous row of color, so it looks like you didn't change colors soon enough. (This happens because when you're knitting in the round, you're actually knitting a spiral, not a circle.) In *Meg Swansen's Knitting* (Interweave, 1999), Meg offers an ingenious technique for eliminating these jogs when working solid-color stripes of two or more rounds.

Work the first stripe (let's call that color A) for the desired number of rounds, change colors (color B) and knit one round.

Work the first stitch of the second round with color B as follows: Pick up the right side of the stitch in the row below the stitch on the needle (it will be color A), put it on the left needle and knit it together with the first stitch on the needle. You will have worked the first stitch of the round twice, but because you work into the stitch below the one on the needle the second time, you have only worked it for one round and it appears as if it were worked just once.

The jog between the two colors disappears and the beginning of the round for color changes only is shifted one stitch to the left. *Note:* Do not change the position of markers required for the placement of any shaping decreases or increases (such as ones used for waist shaping).

Continue working as many rounds as you want with color B. To change to another color, simple repeat the process, working the first stitch of the round a second time by picking up the stitch in the row below the stitch on the needle and knitting it together with the first stitch on the needle, thereby shifting the beginning of the round one more stitch to the left for color changes.

Finished Size
53" (134.5 cm) wide and 23¼" (59 cm) deep at center point, after blocking.

Yarn
The Fibre Company Canopy Worsted (50% alpaca, 30% merino, 20% bamboo; 100 yd [91 m]/1.75 oz [50 g]): yerba mate (olive), 4 skeins. Yarn distributed by Kelbourne Woolens.

Needles
Size 9 (5.5 mm): 24" (61 cm) or longer circular (cir) needle.

Notions
Yarn needle; pins for blocking.

Gauge
14 sts and 22 rows = 4" (10 cm) in garter st, after blocking.

---

note

✳ See Glossary for terms you don't know.

Shawl

CO 6 sts. Work Rows 1–28 of Setup chart—19 sts. Work Rows 1–20 of Body Increase chart 6 times, adding 1 more 10-st rep each time, then work Rows 1–12 once more—85 sts. Work Rows 1–20 of Body Decrease chart 6 times, working 1 less 10-st rep each time—25 sts rem. Work Rows 1–37 of End chart—6 sts rem. BO all sts pwise.

Finishing

With tail from CO row, join first and last sts of row (folding ends to WS of work) to form a corner. Work in same way on BO row. Weave in ends. Soak in wool wash and warm water and pin to measurements. 🍃

KATE GAGNON OSBORN is the co-author of *November Knits* and *Vintage Modern Knits* (both from Interweave). She is co-owner of Kelbourne Woolens and lives in Philadelphia, Pennsylvania.

Oscilloscope SHAWL
Kate Gagnon Osborn

This side-to-side shawl is long enough to be styled as a scarf or knotted like a shawlette. Garter stitch creates interest between eyelet bands. The shawl uses lace as building material and as ornament in a way that is harmonious and exciting. Even in heavier yarns, the drape of a lace accessory makes it easy to wear slipped inside a coat or flaunted over the shoulders.

Setup

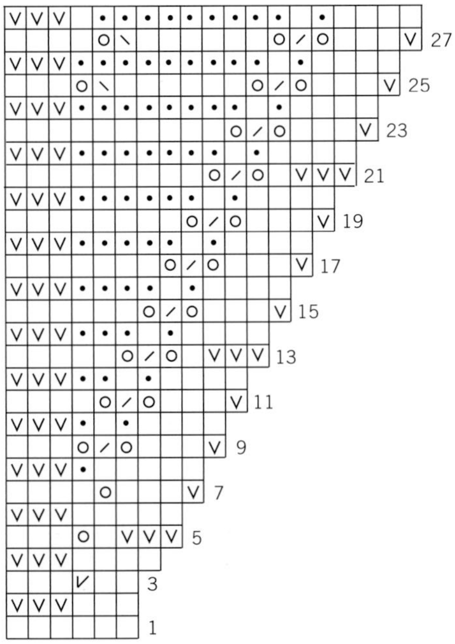
27
25
23
21
19
17
15
13
11
9
7
5
3
1

6 sts

Body increase

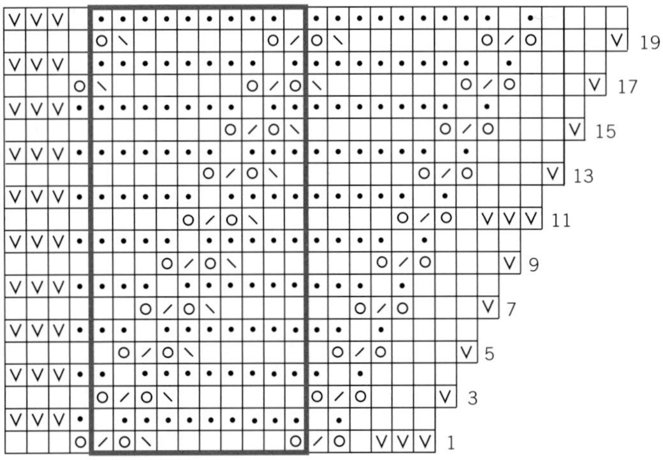
19
17
15
13
11
9
7
5
3
1

10 st repeat

- ☐ k on RS; p on WS
- • p on RS; k on WS
- O yo
- / k2tog
- \ ssk
- V sl 1 wyb on RS; sl 1 wyf on WS
- knit into front and back of same st
- ▢ pattern repeat

Body decrease

10 st repeat

☐	k on RS; p on WS
•	p on RS; k on WS
O	yo
/	k2tog
\	ssk
V	sl 1 wyb on RS; sl 1 wyf on WS
⌵	knit into front and back of same st
☐	pattern repeat

End

Finished Size
46" (117 cm) wide at top edge and 25" (63.5 cm) high at point, after blocking.

Yarn
Imperial Yarn Bulky 2 Strand Pencil Roving (100% wool; 200 yd [183 m]/4 oz [113 g]): #112 wheat heather, 2 balls.

Needles
Size 13 (9 mm). Adjust needle size if necessary to obtain the correct gauge.

Notions
Marker (m); blocking pins; size N/15 (9 mm) crochet hook; smooth waste yarn in contrasting color.

Gauge
9 sts and 10 rows = 4" (10 cm) in leaf lace patt, after blocking.

----

notes

✳ This shawl is worked from the top down.

✳ It may be helpful to mark center stitch.

Shawl

Top border

Using the crochet chain provisional method (see Glossary), CO 3 sts. Knit 6 rows; do not turn after last row. Rotate work and pick up and knit 3 sts down selvedge (1 st between each garter ridge), then gently remove waste yarn from CO sts and place 3 live sts on left needle, k3—9 sts total. Turn.

Pembroke WRAP
Andrea Rangel

Shetland-style lace goes iconic when worked in a bold, chunky gauge. Rendered in light-as-air unspun roving, the fern lace pattern of the Pembroke Wrap has puffy, textural loft. Andrea Rangel uses traditional triangular shawl construction for a familiar piece with modern edge.

SET-UP ROW: (WS) K3 (edge sts), p1, p1 (center st), p1, k3 (edge sts).

Work Rows 1–28 of Set-Up Leaf chart—65 sts; 32 sts each side of center st. Work Rows 1–12 of Leaf Lace chart, working each patt rep 3 times—89 sts; 44 sts each side of center st. Work Rows 1–19 of Arrowhead Scallop Edge chart, working each patt rep 5 times—121 sts; 60 sts each side of center st.

INC ROW: (WS) K3, yo, k4, yo, k1, yo, *k7, yo, k1, yo; rep from * to 4 sts before center st, k4, yo, k1 (center st), yo, k4, yo, k1, yo, *k7, yo, k1, yo; rep from * to last 7 sts, k4, yo, k3—153 sts.

Knit 1 row. BO all sts kwise on WS.

Finishing

Carefully weave in all ends. Block pieces to measurements. 🍃

ANDREA RANGEL loves the functional and artistic nature of fiber arts, especially matching the perfect natural fibers to each project and season. She loves to be (and knit!) outdoors. She teaches, designs, and knits in Seattle, Washington. See her designs at www.andreaknits.com.

	k on RS; p on WS		k2tog
·	k on WS		ssk
O	yo	⋀	sl 2 as if to k2tog, k1, p2sso
			pattern repeat

Set-Up Leaf

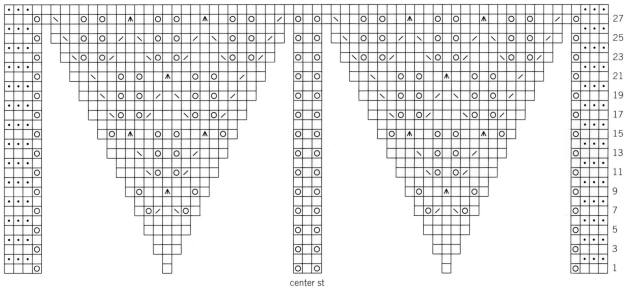

center st

Leaf Lace

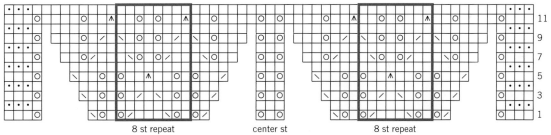

8 st repeat   center st   8 st repeat

Arrowhead Scallop Edge

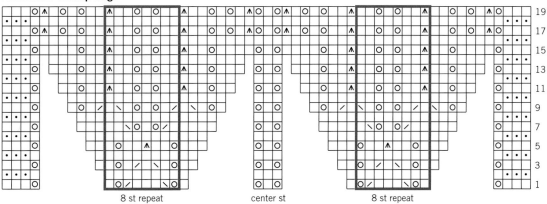

8 st repeat   center st   8 st repeat

Finished Size
5¼" (13.5 cm) wide and 26" (66 cm) long

Yarn
Berroco Blackstone Tweed (65% wool, 25% mohair, 10% angora; 130 yd [119 m]/1.75 oz [50 g]): #2637 plum island, 1 skein

Needles
Size 7 (4.5 mm) needles.

Notions
Yarn needle; four ¾" (2 cm) buttons

Gauge
18 sts and 32 rows (16 ridges) = 4" (10 cm) in garter st

----

notes

* For ease of working, mark the right side with a removable marker or piece of yarn looped through the front of a stitch.

* To count rows in garter stitch, count purl ridges instead of individual rows. One ridge equals two rows of knitting.

* When choosing buttons, bring your project along to make sure that your buttonholes can stretch enough to accommodate the button diameter.

* Sometimes it can be difficult to find buttons with eyes large enough to be sewn with yarn. If that's the case, use a regular sewing needle and matching thread.

Tweed SCARFLET

Sarah Fama

A strip of garter stitch folds and buttons at an angle to make a cowl. The buttonholes are easy—choosing buttons will be the hard part.

Scarflet

CO 24 sts. Beg with a RS row (mark this side; see Notes), work in garter st (knit every row) until piece measures 21" (53.5 cm) from CO—about 84 garter ridges. End with a WS row, so next row will be on RS.

BUTTONHOLE ROW: (RS) K4, yo, k2tog, k12, ssk, yo, k4—2 buttonholes; no change in st count.

Knit 31 rows, ending with a WS row. Work buttonhole row once more. Knit 7 rows. BO all sts.

Finishing

Block to measurements. Sew buttons on RS of scarflet, on end opposite buttonholes, taking care to align the buttons with the buttonholes. Weave in ends. 🍃

SARA FAMA lives in the California Bay area with her husband, son, and neurotic Chihuahua-terrier mix.

Tip

After knitting the stitch before the yarnover, bring the yarn forward between the needle tips. When you knit the next stitch, bring the yarn up and over the right-hand needle to the back of the work again, ready to knit the next stitch. The strand that travels over the top of the needle is the yarnover, and it counts as one stitch.

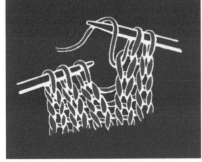

Floating Spiral HAT
Owen Biesel

Deeply textured yarn stands out in high relief in this subtly spiraling hat pattern, perfect for men or women.

Finished Size
24" (61 cm) brim circumference.

Yarn
Debbie Bliss Donegal Luxury Tweed (85% wool, 15% angora; 96 yd [88 m]/1.75 oz [50 g]): #8 green, 2 skeins. Yarn distributed by Knitting Fever.

Needles
Size 8 (5 mm): 16" (40.5 cm) circular (cir) and set of 5 double-pointed needles (dpn). Adjust needle size if necessary to obtain the correct gauge.

Notions
Marker (m); cable needle (cn); tapestry needle.

Gauge
18 sts and 24 rows = 4" (10 cm) in St st; 14 sts and 28 rows = 4" (10 cm) in 1×1 rib (stretched); 30 sts and 32 rows = 4" (10 cm) in cable patt.

---

note

* Moving the marker as directed on Round 3 of the cable pattern is essential to keeping in pattern, as the cables cross over the ends of rounds, forcing the beginning of the rounds to shift.

---

stitch guide

1×1 Rib (multiple of 2 sts)
Rnd 1: *K1, p1; rep from * around.

Rep Rnd 1 for patt.

Cable Pattern (multiple of 10 sts)
Rnds 1, 2, and 4: Knit.

Rnd 3: K5, *k2, sl 3 sts to cn and hold in front, k3, k3 from cn, k2; rep from * to 5 sts before m, k2, sl 3 sts to cn and hold in front, remove m, k3, k3 from cn, k2, pm.

Rep Rnds 1–4 for patt.

Hat

Brim

With cir needle and using the tubular method (see Glossary) for 1×1 rib, CO 94 sts. Place marker (pm) and join in the rnd. Work in 1×1 rib (see Stitch Guide) until piece measures 1" (2.5 cm) from CO.

Crown

SET-UP RND: *K2, M1; rep from * to last 2 sts, k2—140 sts.

Work Rnds 1–4 of cable patt (see Stitch Guide) until piece measures 4" (10 cm) from CO, ending with Rnd 4.

Shape crown, changing to dpn when necessary:

RND 1: Knit.

RND 2: (dec rnd) *K8, [k2tog] 2 times, k8; rep from * around—126 sts rem.

RND 3: K7, sl 2 sts to cn and hold in front, k2, k2 from cn, *k4, sl 3 sts to cn and hold in front, k3, k3 from cn, k4, sl 2 sts to cn and hold in front, k2, k2 from cn; rep from * to last 7 sts, k4, sl 3 sts to cn and hold in front, remove m, k3, k3 from cn, k2, pm.

RNDS 4 AND 5: Knit.

RND 6: (dec rnd) *K5, k2tog, k4, k2tog, k5; rep from * around—112 sts rem.

RND 7: K6, sl 2 sts to cn and hold in front, k2, k2 from cn, *k3, sl 3 sts to cn and hold in front, k3, k3 from cn, k3, sl 2 sts to cn and hold in front, k2, k2 from cn; rep from * to last 6 sts, k3, sl 3 sts to cn and hold

in front, remove m, k3, k3 from cn, k2, pm.

RNDS 8 AND 9: Knit.

RND 10: (dec rnd) *K6, [k2tog] 2 times, k6; rep from * around—98 sts rem.

RND 11: K6, sl 1 st to cn and hold in front, k1, k1 from cn, *k3, sl 3 sts to cn and hold in front, k3, k3 from cn, k3, sl 1 st to cn and hold in front, k1, k1 from cn; rep from * to last 6 sts, k3, sl 3 sts to cn and hold in front, remove m, k3, k3 from cn, k2, pm.

RNDS 12 AND 13: Knit.

RND 14: (dec rnd) *K4, k2tog, k2, k2tog, k4; rep from * around—84 sts rem.

RND 15: K5, sl 1 st to cn and hold in front, k1, k1 from cn, *k2, sl 3 sts to cn and hold in front, k3, k3 from cn, k2, sl 1 st to cn and hold in front, k1, k1 from cn; rep from * to last 5 sts, k2, sl 3 sts to cn and hold

in front, remove m, k3, k3 from cn, k2, pm.

RNDS 16 AND 17: Knit.

RND 18: (dec rnd) *[K2tog] 2 times, k8; rep from * around—70 sts rem.

RND 19: Work Rnd 3 of cable patt.

RNDS 20 AND 21: Knit.

RND 22: Work Rnd 3 of cable patt.

RND 23: (dec rnd) *K2tog, k8; rep from * around—63 sts rem.

RND 24: K2, *k4, sl 3 sts to cn and hold in front, k2, (k2tog, k1) from cn; rep from * to last 7 sts, k4, sl 3 sts to cn and hold in front, remove m, k2, (k2tog, k1) from cn, k2, pm—56 sts rem.

RND 25: (dec rnd) *K2tog, k6; rep from * around—49 sts rem.

RND 26: (dec rnd) K2, *k2, sl 3 sts to cn and hold in front, k2, (k2tog, k1) from cn; rep from * to last 5 sts, k2, sl 3 sts to cn and hold in front, remove m, k2, (k2tog, k1) from cn, k1, pm—42 sts rem.

RND 27: (dec rnd) *K2tog, k4; rep from * around—35 sts rem.

RND 28: (dec rnd) K1, *k2, sl 2 sts to cn and hold in front, k1, k2tog from cn; rep from * to last 4 sts, k2, sl 2 sts to cn and hold in front, remove m, k1, k2tog from cn, k1, pm—28 sts rem.

RND 29: (dec rnd) *K2tog, k2; rep from * around—21 sts rem.

RND 30: (dec rnd) K1, *sl 2 sts to cn and hold in front, k1, k2tog from cn; rep from * to last 2 sts, sl 2 sts to cn and hold in front, remove m, k1, k2tog from cn, k1—14 sts rem.

RND 31: (dec rnd) [K2tog] 7 times—7 sts rem.

Break yarn and thread tail through rem sts. Cinch to close. Weave in all loose ends. 🌿

Just a few years ago, **OWEN BIESEL** learned to knit from his grandmother, and he quickly fell in love with the craft. Now a graduate student in mathematics, he still finds time to knit and create his own designs.

Flamboyant SHAWL
Maria Leigh

The Flamboyant Shawl is a small crescent in plush garter stitch with a rippled edge.

Finished Size
56½" (143.5 cm) from tip to tip and 11½" (29 cm) at widest point.

Yarn
Manos del Uruguay Rittenhouse Merino 5-ply (100% extrafine merino; 240 yd [220 m]/3.5 oz [100 g]): #509 maroon, 2 hanks. Yarn distributed by Fairmount Fibers.

Needles
Size 7 (4.5 mm): 29" (73.5 cm) circular (cir) needle. Adjust needle size if necessary to obtain the correct gauge.

Notions
Tapestry needle.

Gauge
18 sts and 32 rows = 4" (10 cm) in garter st.

----

notes

* This shawl is worked in garter stitch from tip to tip, increasing stitches to center point, and then decreasing stitches to end. Stitches are picked up along one long shaped edge for ruffle.

* Ruffle is shaped using short-rows. Because the short-rows are worked in garter stitch, there is no need to work the wraps together with the wrapped stitches.

* Piece is worked back and forth in rows. A circular needle is used to accommodate the large number of stitches.

* Slip stitches at beginning of wrong-side rows purlwise with yarn in front. Bring yarn to back of work again before knitting the next stitch.

Shawl

Using the long-tail method, CO 3 sts. Do not join. Work incs:

ROWS 1, 3, AND 5: (WS) Sl 1 (see Notes), k2.

ROWS 2 AND 4: Knit.

ROW 6: (RS) Knit to last 2 sts, k1f&b, k1—1 st inc'd.

ROWS 7, 9, AND 11: Sl 1, knit to end.

ROWS 8 AND 10: Knit.

Rep Rows 6–11 thirty-six more times, ending with a WS row—40 sts. Work decs:

ROW 1: (RS) Knit to last 3 sts, k2tog, k1—1 st dec'd.

ROWS 2, 4, AND 6: Sl 1, knit to end.

ROWS 3 AND 5: Knit.

Rep Rows 1–6 thirty-six more times, ending with a WS row—3 sts rem.

Shape ruffle

NEXT ROW: (RS) K1, k2tog, turn piece clockwise and work [k1, p1] into each slipped st along long shaped edge, turn piece clockwise and pick up and knit 2 sts along CO edge—454 sts total. Do not join.

Beg short-rows *(see Glossary)*

SHORT-ROWS 1 AND 2: Knit to last 16 sts, wrap next st, turn.

SHORT-ROW 3: Knit to 16 sts before wrapped st, wrap next st, turn.

Rep Row 3 eleven more times, ending with a RS row.

Knit 3 rows across all sts. BO all sts.

Finishing

Block piece to measurements. Weave in ends. 🍃

MARIA LEIGH is a fashion designer and avid knitter. She has relocated from Korea and lives in Ontario, Canada, with her husband and her cat, Tarae (which means "yarn ball" in Korean). She blogs at www.amigurumikr.com.

Conifer SHAWL
Kate Gagnon Osborn

This top-down shawl increases at the regular rate of four stitches every other row. Three pattern sections are flanked by garter edges, and the center stitch is worked in stockinette throughout. A worsted-weight yarn makes for a substantial fabric in a small silhouette.

Finished Size

48" (122 cm) wide at top and 23" (58.5 cm) deep after blocking.

Yarn

The Fibre Company Canopy Worsted (50% alpaca, 30% merino, 20% bamboo; 100 yd [91 m]/1.75 oz [50 g]): chiclet tree, 5 skeins. Yarn distributed by Kelbourne Woolens.

Needles

Size 8 (5 mm): 36" (91.5 cm) circular (cir) needle.

Notions

Waste yarn; marker (m); cable needle (cn); yarn needle.

Gauge

17 sts and 24 rows = 4" (10 cm) in lattice patt after blocking.

notes

✳ See Glossary for terms you don't know.

✳ To work the Lattice, Conifer, and Edging charts, work the first half of the chart to the center stitch, working the repeat box as many times as needed, then work the second half of the chart, working the second repeat box the same number of times as the first. It is helpful to place a marker before the center stitch.

Shawl

With waste yarn and the invisible-provisional method, CO 2 sts. Knit 10 rows.

NEXT ROW: K2, rotate work and pick up and knit 1 st in each of 5 garter ridges, remove waste yarn and transfer live sts to needle, k2 from needle—9 sts.

☐ k on RS; p on WS	⁄ k2tog	▨ no stitch
• p on RS; k on WS	＼ ssk	☐ pattern repeat
○ yo	⋀ sl 2 as if to k2tog, k1, p2sso	

⟩⟨ on WS: sl 2 sts onto cn, hold in back, p2, p2 from cn

⟩⟨ on WS: sl 2 sts onto cn, hold in front, p2, p2 from cn

Set-Up

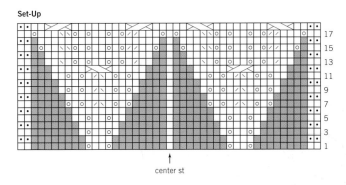

center st

Lattice

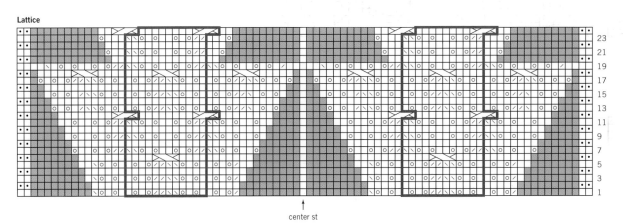

center st

Work Rows 1–18 of Set-Up chart—45 sts. Work Rows 1–24 of Lattice chart 2 times—141 sts. Work Rows 1–12 of Lattice chart once more—165 sts. Work Rows 1–24 of Conifer chart—213 sts. Work Rows 1–11 of Edging chart—237 sts.

With WS facing, loosely BO all sts kwise.

Finishing

Weave in ends. Soak in warm water and wool wash. Pin to measurements and let dry. 🍃

KATE GAGNON OSBORN is the co-author of *November Knits* and *Vintage Modern Knits* (both from Interweave). She is co-owner of Kelbourne Woolens and lives in Philadelphia, Pennsylvania.

Conifer

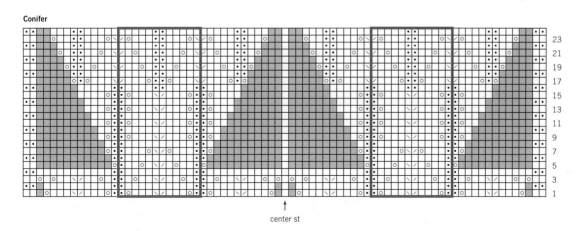

center st

Edging

center st

Extra! Extra! HAT

Annie Modesitt

Annie Modesitt puts a new twist on the traditional newsboy cap. Casual, comfy, and supersoft in Muench Touch Me and Merino Soft.

Finished Size
21 (23)" (53.5 [58.5] cm) head circumference.

Yarn
Muench Touch Me (72% rayon, 28% wool; 61 yd [56 m]/1.75 oz [50 g]): #3607 black (A), 3 balls, all sizes.

Muench Merino Soft (100% superwash merino, 186 yd [170 m]/1.75 oz [50 g]): #15 black (B), 2 balls all sizes.

Needles
Size 8 (5 mm): 16" (40.5 cm) circular needle. Size 5 (3.75 mm): 16" (40.5 cm) circular needle.

Notions
Yarn needle.

Gauge
15 sts and 16 rnds = 4" (10 cm) in St st with 2 strands

---

note

* **Construction Plan:** Cap is worked in the round, using 1 strand of each yarn held together. Crown is shaped in 6 sections using double decreases. The brim is picked up and worked after the hat is finished.

---

stitch guide

Vertical Double Decrease (VDD)
Slip 2 sts as if to k2tog, k1, pass slipped sts over knit st (centered double decrease).

HAT

With larger circular needle and 1 strand of each yarn held tog, CO 81 (93) sts. Knit 1 WS row.

Horizontal I-Cord

(RS) *K1f&b, k1, k2tog tbl, return 3 sts from right needle to left needle; rep from * until, after returning 3 sts to left needle, there are 5 sts on left needle, end k1, VDD, k1, return 2 sts to left needle, k2tog tbl—78 (90) sts rem.

Headband

Join for working in the rnd, being careful not to twist sts; place marker (pm) for beg of rnd.

RND 1: *K13 (15), pm; rep from * to end.

RND 2: *K6 (7), sl 1, k6 (7); rep from * to end.

RND 3: *K2 (3), M1, knit to 2 (3) sts before next m, M1, k2 (3); rep from * to end.

RND 4: *K7 (8), sl 1, k7 (8); rep from * to end.

RND 5: Rep Rnd 3.

RND 6: *K8 (9), sl 1, k8 (9); rep from * to end.

RNDS 7, 9, 11, 13, AND 15: Knit.

RND 8: *K7 (8), yo, k1, sl 1, k1, yo, k7 (8); rep from * to end.

RND 10: *K8 (9), yo, k1, sl 1, k1, yo, k8 (9); rep from * to end.

RND 12: *K9 (10), yo, k1, sl 1, k1, yo, k9 (10); rep from * to end.

RNDS 14 AND 16: *K11 (12), sl 1, k11 (12); rep from * to end.

RND 17: Knit.

You should have 138 (150) sts.

Crown

RND 1: Purl.

All even-numbered rnds Knit.

RND 3: *K10 (11), VDD, k11 (10), pm; rep from * to end.

RND 5: *K10 (11), sl 1, k11 (10); rep from * to end.

RND 7: *K9 (10), VDD, k10 (9); rep from * to end.

RND 9: *K9 (10), sl 1, k10 (9); rep from * to end.

RND 11: *K8 (9), VDD, k9 (8); rep from * to end.

RND 13: *K8 (9), sl 1, k9 (8); rep from * to end.

RND 15: *K7 (8), VDD, k8 (7); rep from * to end.

RND 17: *K7 (8), sl 1, k8 (7); rep from * to end.

RND 19: *K6 (7), VDD, k7 (6); rep from * to end.

RND 21: *K6 (7), sl 1, k7 (6); rep from * to end.

RND 23: *K5 (6), VDD, k6 (5); rep from * to end.

RND 25: *K5 (6), sl 1, k6 (5); rep from * to end.

RND 27: *K4 (5), VDD, k5 (4); rep from * to end.

RND 29: *K4 (5), sl 1, k5 (4); rep from * to end.

RND 31: *K3 (4), VDD, k4 (3); rep from * to end.

RND 33: *K3 (4), sl 1, k4 (3); rep from * to end.

RND 35: *K2 (3), VDD, k3 (2); rep from * to end.

RND 37: *K2 (3), sl 1, k3 (2); rep from * to end.

RND 39: *K1 (2), VDD, k2 (1); rep from * to end.

RND 41: *K1 (2), sl 1, k2 (1); rep from * to end.

RND 43: *K0 (1), VDD, k1 (0); rep from * to end.

Size 23" (58.5 cm) only

RND 45: *K1, sl 1, k1; rep from * to end.

RND 47: [VDD] 6 times.

Both sizes

For both sizes, 6 sts rem. Cut yarn, leaving a 12" (30.5 cm) tail. Run yarn through rem sts, pull tightly to close hole. Fasten off securely.

Brim

With RS facing, smaller circular needle, 1 strand of A and 2 strands of B, pick up and knit 75 (81) sts along CO edge, near the lower edge of the horizontal I-cord. Turn so WS is facing and work short-rows as follows:

Left side

SHORT-ROW 1: P1, wrap next st and turn, k1.

SHORT-ROW 2: P2, wrap next st and turn, k2.

SHORT-ROW 3: P3, wrap next st and turn, knit to end.

SHORT-ROW 4: P4, wrap next st and turn, knit to end.

SHORT-ROW 5: P5, wrap next st and turn, knit to end.

NEXT ROW: (WS) Purl across all sts.

Right side

Beg with RS facing, work short-rows as follows:

SHORT-ROW 1: K1, wrap next st and turn, p1.

SHORT-ROW 2: K2, wrap next st and turn, p2.

SHORT-ROW 3: K3, wrap next st and turn, purl to end.

SHORT-ROW 4: K4, wrap next st and turn, purl to end.

SHORT-ROW 5: K5, wrap next st and turn, purl to end.

NEXT ROW: (RS) Knit across all sts.

Front edge

Work 3 (3) rows even in St st (knit RS rows, purl WS rows).

NEXT ROW: (RS) Knit to last 8 sts, wrap next st and turn.

NEXT ROW: (WS) Purl to last 12 sts, wrap next st and turn.

NEXT ROW: (RS) Knit to last 16 sts, wrap next st and turn.

NEXT ROW: (WS) Purl to last 16 sts, wrap next st and turn.

NEXT ROW: (RS) Knit, working wraps tog with wrapped sts as k2tog; at end of row, pick up and knit 6 sts along original short-row edge of brim—81 (87) sts.

TURNING ROW: (WS) Knit all sts, working rem wraps tog with wrapped sts; at end of row, pick up and knit 6 sts along original short-row edge of brim—87 (93) sts total.

NEXT ROW: (RS) Purl.

Work even in rev St st (purl RS rows, knit WS rows) for 4 rows. With larger needle, BO all sts.

FINISHING

Turn rev St st edge under, folding it at point where work changes from St st to rev St st. With a single strand of B and yarn needle, tack in place. Tack brim at each side to lower edge of cap at horizontal I-cord. Weave in ends. Block cap by slipping a plate into the hat and steaming. Steam-block the brim, shaping it with your hands to desired dimensions. ✐

ANNIE MODESITT is a St. Paul–based designer. She loves all types of fiber, biking, snow, and her family—though not in that order. She has taught all over the United States and at a few places in Europe, too. She's lucky.

> **Tip**
>
> Brim is shaped with short-rows (see Glossary). Be sure to work wrap together with wrapped stitch as k2tog or p2tog the next time you work across the wrap.

Finished Size
5½" (14 cm) wrist circumference, 7½" (19 cm) cuff circumference, and 9½" (24 cm) long from wrist to cuff, relaxed.

Yarn
Manos del Uruguay Wool Clásica (100% wool; 138 yd [126 m]/3.5 oz [100 g]): #69 hibiscus, 1 skein. Yarn distributed by Fairmount Fibers.

Needles
Size 9 (5.5 mm): set of double-pointed needles (dpn).

Notions
Markers (m) in three colors; cable needle (cn); yarn needle; size I/9 (5.5 mm) crochet hook (optional).

Gauge
17 sts and 24 rows = 4" (10 cm) in St st.

---

notes

* See Glossary for terms you don't know.

* The cast-on edge makes one side of the triangle at the top of the hand. After the triangle is shaped using short-rows, additional stitches for the wrist are cast on, and the remainder of the piece is worked in the round.

* The placement of the markers is essential to this pattern. There are three markers to keep track of: the beginning-of-round marker (BRM), the mid-round marker (MRM), and the design marker (DM). These markers will be so abbreviated throughout.

---

stitch guide

Left Twist (LT)
Sl next st onto cn and hold in front, k1, k1 from cn.

Left Purl Twist (LPT)
Sl next st onto cn and hold in front, p1, k1 from cn.

Right Twist (RT)
Sl next st onto cn and hold in back, k1, k1 from cn.

Right Purl Twist (RPT)
Sl next st onto cn and hold in back, k1, p1 from cn.

Axiomatic MITTS

Jenna Hurry

Top-down mitts feature 1×1 ribbed sections shaped with short-rows. A crochet finger loop keeps everything in place.

Left Mitt

CO 17 sts, leaving an 85" (216 cm) tail for optional crochet edging if desired. Do not join; work back and forth on 2 dpn.

ROWS 1 AND 3: (RS) *K1, p1; rep from * to laSt st, k1.

ROW 2: (WS) *P1, k1; rep from * to last 3 sts, p1, place marker (pm), wrap next st, turn.

ROW 4: *P1, k1; rep from * to 3 sts before m, p1, pm, wrap next st, turn.

Rep Rows 3 and 4 five more times, then rep Row 3 once more.

Left wrist

RND 1: (WS) Work in patt across all sts, working wraps tog with wrapped sts and removing m. At end of row, turn so RS is facing and use the knitted method to CO 11 sts at beg of row, then cont as foll: *P1, k1; rep from * 5 more times, [RPT (see Stitch Guide)] 6 times, RT (see Stitch Guide), place BRM (see Notes), k2, join for working in the rnd—28 sts total.

RND 2 (FIRST 2 STS ALREADY WORKED): *P1, k1; rep from * 5 more times, place MRM (see Notes), [k1, p1] 6 times, k2.

RND 3: K1, place DM (see Notes), LT (see Stitch Guide), [LPT (see Stitch Guide)] 5 times, k1, sl MRM, k1, [RPT] 5 times, RT, place DM, k1.

First slant

RND 4: Knit to DM, remove DM, k1, place DM, [k1, p1] to 2 sts before MRM, k4, [p1, k1] to 1 st before DM, place DM, k1, remove DM, knit to end.

RND 5: Knit to DM, LT, [LPT] to MRM, [RPT] to 2 sts before DM, RT, knit to end.

RND 6: Knit to DM, remove DM, k1, place DM, [k1, p1] to 1 st before MRM, k2, [p1, k1] to 1 st before DM, place DM, k1, remove DM, knit to end.

RND 7: Knit to DM, LT, [LPT] to 1 st before MRM, k2, [RPT] to 2 sts before DM, RT, knit to end.

Rep Rnds 4–7 three more times—5 sts rem between DM and MRM. Rep Rnds 4–6 once more. *At the same time*, inc 2 sts on 7th rnd of first slant (second "Rnd 6") as foll: K1, M1, knit to DM, remove DM, k1, place DM, [k1, p1] to 1 st before MRM, k2, [p1, k1] to 1 st before DM, place DM, k1, remove DM, knit to laSt st, M1, k1—30 sts. After first slant is complete, cont as foll:

Peak

RND 1: Knit to DM, LT, k2, RT, knit to end.

RND 2: Knit to DM, remove DM, k1, place DM, k4, place DM, k1, remove DM, knit to end.

RND 3: Knit to DM, LT, RT, knit to end.

RND 4: Knit to DM, remove DM, knit to DM, remove DM, knit to end.

INC RND: Knit to 1 st before MRM, M1, k2, M1, knit to end—32 sts. Knit 3 rnds.

Second slant

RND 1: LT, place DM, knit to last 2 sts, place DM, RT.

RND 2: Knit to DM, remove DM, k1, place DM, knit to 1 st before DM, place DM, k1, remove DM, knit to end.

RND 3: K1, LT, sl DM, knit to DM, RT, k1.

RND 4: Rep Rnd 2.

RND 5: LT, [LPT] to DM, knit to DM, [RPT] to last 2 sts, RT.

RND 6: K2, [p1, k1] to DM, remove DM, k1, place DM, knit to 1 st before DM, place DM, k1, remove DM, [k1, p1] to last 2 sts, k2.

RND 7: K1, LT, [LPT] to DM, knit to DM, [RPT] to last 3 sts, RT, k1.

RND 8: K3, [p1, k1] to DM, remove DM, k1, place DM, knit to 1 st before DM, place DM, k1, remove DM, [k1, p1] to last 3 sts, k3.

Rep Rnds 5–8 two more times—10 sts between BRM and DM. *At the same time*, inc 2 sts on 13th rnd of 2nd slant as foll: LT, [LPT] to DM, knit to 1 st before MRM, M1, k2, M1, knit to DM, [RPT] to last 2 sts, RT—34 sts. When 2nd slant is complete, cont as foll:

Rib

RND 1: LT, [LPT] to DM, [p1, k1] to DM, [RPT] to last 2 sts, RT.

RND 2: K2, [p1, k1] to DM, remove DM, k1, place DM, [k1, p1] to 1 st before DM, place DM, k1, remove DM, [k1, p1] to last 2 sts, k2.

RND 3: K1, LT, [LPT] to DM, [k1, p1] to DM, [RPT] to last 3 sts, RT, k1.

RND 4: K3, [p1, k1] to DM, remove DM, k1, place DM, [k1, p1] to 1 st before DM, place DM, p1, remove DM, [k1, p1] to last 3 sts, k3.

Rep Rnds 1–4 once more. BO all sts loosely in patt.

Right Mitt

CO 17 sts, leaving an 85" (216 cm) tail for optional crochet edging if desired. Do not join; work back and forth on 2 dpn.

ROWS 1 AND 3: (WS) *P1, k1; rep from * to last st, p1.

ROW 2: (RS) *K1, p1; rep from * to last 3 sts, k1, pm, wrap next st, turn.

ROW 4: *K1, p1; rep from * to 3 sts before m, k1, pm, wrap next st, turn.

Rep Rows 3 and 4 five more times, then rep Row 3 once more.

Wrist set-up

(RS) Work in patt across all sts, working wraps tog with wrapped sts and removing m. At end of row, turn so WS is facing and use the knitted method to CO 11 sts—28 sts total. Turn so RS is facing and join for working in the rnd.

Wrist

RND 1: K1, p1, place BRM, place DM, LT, [LPT] 6 times, place MRM, [k1, p1] to 2 sts before BRM, k2, place DM—2 sts shifted; rnd now beg at BRM.

RND 2: Remove DM, k1, place DM, [k1, p1] to 1 st before MRM, k2, [p1, k1] to 1 st before DM, place DM, k1, remove DM.

RND 3: K1, sl DM, LT, [LPT] to 1 st before MRM, k2, [RPT] to 2 sts before DM, RT, k1.

Beg with first slant, work and finish as for left mitt.

Finishing

Optional crochet edging

At peak of triangle, use tail to chain 12 (or as many as necessary to reach around the middle finger and back to the tip of the triangle), then work sc around entire top opening. Fasten off. To wear, twist the chain loop once and pass over the middle finger. Weave in ends. 🖊

JENNA HURRY has a website at www .knitsandwovens.com, where the latest FibreSpark Knits & Wovens patterns appear, along with a link to her blog.

Finished Size
7 (9)" (18 [23] cm) foot circumference,
17¼ (15)" (44 [38] cm) long from CO to
tip of toe; to fit a woman's small (large).

Yarn
Louet Gems Worsted (100% merino; 175 yd (160 m)/3.5 oz [100 g]):
2 skeins, shown in pampas grass and
mustard. **Note:** The small socks, as
shown, only required a small amount of
the second skein.

Needles
Size 7 (4.5 mm) double-pointed needles
(dpn).

Notions
Yarn needle.

Gauge
13 sts and 17 rnds = 2" (5 cm) in patt
st in the rnd.

---

note

* See Glossary for terms you don't know.

---

stitch guide

Right Twist (RT)
K2tog but leave sts on left needle, then
knit the first st again and sl both sts off
needle.

Sock

Cuff

Loosely CO 44 (52) sts and distrib-
ute them over 4 dpn as foll: 12 (16)
sts on Needle 1, 12 sts on Needle 2,
12 sts on Needle 3, and 8 (12) sts on
Needle 4. Join for working in the
rnd; rnd beg at the side of the leg.
Work in rib as foll: *K2, p2; rep from
* to end of rnd. Rep this rnd 3 more
times—4 rnds of rib total.

Leg

RND 1: *RT (see Stitch Guide), k2; rep
from * to end of rnd.

RND 2: Knit.

RND 3: *K2, RT; rep from * to end of
rnd.

RND 4: Knit.

Rep Rnds 1–4 until piece measures
about 13 (15)" (33 [38] cm) from CO
or about 2 (2¼)" (5 [5.5] cm) less than
desired total length, ending with Rnd
2 or 4.

First-Time TUBE SOCKS
Ann Budd

If you've never knitted a pair of socks, give these tube
socks a try. With no heel or gusset shaping, they knit up
as effortlessly as a stocking cap. The easy-to-memorize
stitch pattern provides structure and elasticity. Sized to fit a
child's/woman's small (woman's large/man's) foot.

Toe

Rearrange sts so that there are 11 (13) sts on each needle and so that the rnd beg between Needles 1 and 4.

RND 1: Needle 1: K1, ssk, knit to end; Needle 2: knit to last 3 sts, k2tog, k1; Needle 3: k1, ssk, knit to end; Needle 4: knit to last 3 sts, k2tog, k1—4 sts dec'd.

Rnd 2 Knit.

Rep Rnds 1 and 2 until 20 (24) sts rem. Then rep Rnd 1 every rnd until 8 sts rem. Cut yarn, leaving a 6–8" (15–20.5 cm) tail. Thread tail on a yarn needle, draw through rem sts twice, and pull tight to close toe. Fasten off.

Finishing

Weave in ends. Dampen socks and lay flat to block. 🌿

ANN BUDD is a freelance editor, designer, and author who lives in Boulder, Colorado, and teaches knitting workshops around the country. Learn more about her at annbuddknits.com.

Subway MITTENS
Colleen Meagher

Colleen Meagher accents the Subway Mittens with a pocket perfectly sized for a mass-transit system's pass card. A twisted-rib cuff seals out the wind.

Finished Size

8" (20.5 cm) hand circumference and 10½" (26.5 cm) long from cuff CO to tip of fingers. To fit a woman's medium to large hand.

Yarn

Cascade 220 (100% wool; 220 yd [201 m]/3.5 oz [100 g]): #4008 maroon, 1 skein.

Needles

Sizes 5 (3.75 mm) and 7 (4.5 mm): double-pointed needles (dpn). Adjust needle size if necessary to obtain the correct gauge.

Notions

Markers (m); one ¾" (2 cm) button; tapestry needle.

Gauge

20 sts and 28 rows = 4" (10 cm) in St st in the rnd on larger needles.

Mitten

Cuff

With smaller dpn, CO 40 sts. Place marker (pm) and join for working in the rnd.

NEXT RND: *K1, p1; rep from * around.

NEXT RND: *K1 through back loop (k1tbl), p1; rep from * around.

Rep last 2 rows until piece measures 3" (7.5 cm) from CO.

Hand

Change to larger dpn. Knit 1 rnd.

Thumb gusset

K19, pm, M1L (see Glossary), k1, M1R (see Glossary), pm, knit to end—2 sts inc'd. Cont in St st, inc 2

sts between markers in this manner every 3 rows 4 more times, then every 4 rows 1 time—13 gusset sts.

NEXT RND: Knit to first gusset m, remove m, place 13 gusset sts on a piece of waste yarn, use the backward-loop method (see Glossary) to CO 1 st over gap, remove second m, knit to end of rnd—40 sts rem for hand.

Work even in St st in the rnd for 6" (15 cm), or until knitting reaches top of pinky finger.

Shape top

*K8, k2tog; rep from * 3 more times—36 sts rem. Knit 1 rnd.

NEXT RND: *K7, k2tog; rep from * 3 more times—32 sts rem. Knit 1 rnd.

NEXT RND: *K6, k2tog; rep from * 3 more times—28 sts rem.

Knit 1 rnd. Cont to dec every other rnd in this manner until 8 sts rem. Break yarn and draw through rem sts. Secure tail to WS of mitten.

Thumb

Transfer 13 held sts to larger dpn, distributing them evenly over 3 needles. Join yarn, pick up and knit 1 st in gap above thumb sts, then knit around all sts and join for working in the rnd—14 sts total. Work in St st until thumb measures 3½" (9 cm) or desired length to top of thumb.

Shape thumb

RND 1: K5, [k2tog] 2 times, knit to end—12 sts rem.

RND 2: *Ssk (see Glossary), k2, k2tog; rep from * 1 time—8 sts rem.

RND 3: Knit.

RND 4: K3, [k2tog] 2 times, k1—6 sts rem.

RND 5: K1, [k2tog] 2 times, k1—4 sts rem.

Break yarn and thread through rem sts. Secure tail to WS.

Finishing

Transit card pocket

Measure the size of your transit card. Pocket shown was designed for a 2⅛" × 3⅜" (5.3 × 8.5 cm) card. If needed, adjust pocket directions to fit your card.

Pocket

With larger dpn, CO 12 sts. Work in St st in rows for 3½" (9 cm). BO all sts.

Flap

With larger dpn, CO 14 sts.

NEXT ROW: (RS) Knit.

NEXT ROW: (WS) K2, p10, k2.

Rep last 2 rows 4 more times. Cont garter st edges and dec as foll:

ROW 1: (RS) K2, ssk, knit to last 4 sts, k2tog, k2—2 sts dec'd.

ROW 2: (WS) K2, purl to last 2 sts, k2.

Rep last 2 rows 2 more times—8 sts rem.

Buttonhole

ROW 1: (RS) K2, BO 4 sts, k2.

ROW 2: (WS) K2, use the backward-loop method to CO 4 sts, k2.

Work 1 WS row in patt. BO all sts. Sew bottom edge of pocket to top of hand of right mitten. Use mattress st (see Glossary) to sew sides of pocket in place. Sew flap to mitten about ½" (1.3 cm) above top of pocket. Sew button to pocket opposite butthonhole. Weave in loose ends. 🍃

COLLEEN MEAGHER designed these mittens for Boston's transit system pass. More recently she's moved to New York City, where she can enjoy much longer subway rides. Read more at www.subwayknitter.com.

Finished Size
9¼" (23.5 cm) wide and 78" (198 cm) long.

Yarn
Tahki Sedona Hand Dyed (90% merino; 10% silk; 108 yd [100 m]/1.75 oz [50 g]): #20 dark gray blend, 5 skeins.

Needles
Size 6 (4 mm) needles.

Notions
Yarn needle.

Gauge
22 sts and 28 rows = 4" (10 cm) in rib patt, slightly stretched.

Scarf
CO 51 sts.

ROW 1: K2, p3, k5, p2, k2, p6, k3, p4, k2, p5, k6, p2, k4, p3, k2.

ROW 2: P2, k3, p4, k2, p6, k5, p2, k4, p3, k6, p2, k2, p5, k3, p2.

Rep Rows 1 and 2 until piece measures 78" (198 cm) or desired length from CO. BO all sts in rib.

Finishing
Block to measurements. Weave in ends. 🍂

> **Tip**
>
> Pause to check which row you're on when starting a new row. Row 1 of the pattern should have knit stitches at both ends; Row 2 should have purl stitches at both ends. If the first two stitches at the beginning of the row are knit stitches, it's time to work Row 1. If they are purl stitches, it's time to work Row 2. Once you've worked a couple inches, you should be able to work the stitches without following the pattern—work the stitches as they appear! Knit the knit stitches and purl the purl stitches.

Irregular Rib SCARF
Kenny Chua

Mix up knits and purls to make a simple ribbed scarf. An irregular pattern will help you learn to read your knitting.

Elfin Hat AND Scarf Set

Cathy Carron

A yarn with a hint of camel adds a little luxury to Cathy Carron's easy mesh-stitch Elfin Hat and Scarf Set. Deep ribs give a finished look.

Finished Size
Hat: 16" (40.5 cm) head circumference.
Scarf: 7¾" (19.5 cm) wide and 42" (106.5 cm) long.

Yarn
Knit One Crochet Too Camelino (90% merino, 10% camel; 109 yd [100 m]/1.75 oz [50 g]): #256 lipstick (red). **Hat:** 3 skeins. **Scarf:** 3 skeins.

Needles
Hat: Size 7 (4.5 mm): set of double-pointed (dpn) and 16" (40.5 cm) circular (cir) needles. **Scarf:** Size 7 (4.5 mm): straight needles. Adjust needle size if necessary to obtain the correct gauge.

Notions
Markers (m); pom-pom maker; tapestry needle.

Gauge
20 sts and 32 rows = 4" (10 cm) in mesh patt.

Scarf

CO 40 sts.

NEXT ROW: *K2, p2; rep from * to end. Cont in 2×2 rib until piece measures 4½" (11.5 cm) from CO.

RNDS 1, 3, AND 4: Knit.

RND 2: K2, *yo, k2tog; rep from * to last 2 sts, k2.

Rep Rnds 1–4 until piece measures 33" (84 cm) from CO. Work in 2×2 rib for 4½" (11.5 cm). BO all sts in rib. Weave in ends.

Hat

CO 12 sts. Divide sts over 3 dpn—4 sts each needle. Place marker (pm) and join for working in the rnd.

RNDS 1, 5, 9, 13, AND 17: Purl.

RNDS 2, 6, 10, 14, AND 18: Knit.

RND 3: *K1, yo, k2tog, k1; rep from * around.

RND 4: *K4, M1 (see Glossary); rep from * around—15 sts.

RND 7: *K1, [yo, k2tog] 2 times; rep from * around.

RND 8: *K5, M1; rep from * around—18 sts.

RND 11: *K1, [yo, k2tog] 2 times, k1; rep from * around.

RND 12: *K6, M1; rep from * around—21 sts.

RND 15: *K1, [yo, k2tog] 3 times; rep from * around.

RND 16: *K7, M1; rep from * around—24 sts.

RND 19: *K1, [yo, k2tog] 3 times, k1; rep from * around.

RND 20: *K8, M1; rep from * around— 27 sts.

Cont in patt, changing to cir needle when necessary. Inc 3 sts on every 4th rnd, working new sts into mesh patt, until there are 96 sts total. End with a purl rnd.

Band

RND 1: Knit.

RND 2: *K2, p2; rep from * around.

Rep Rnd 2 until rib section measures 6" (15 cm). BO all sts in rib.

Finishing

Weave in ends. Make a 3" (7.5 cm) pom-pom (see sidebar). With yarn threaded on a tapestry needle, attach pom-pom to pointed end of hat. Fold up band to wear. 🍂

CATHY CARRON knits everywhere she can, but most often in New York City and in the Connecticut countryside. She is the author of *Knitting Sweaters From the Top Down* (Lark, 2007).

Pom-Pom

Cut two circles of cardboard, each ½" (1.3 cm) larger than desired finished pom-pom width. Cut a small circle out of the center and a small edge out of the side of each circle **(figure 1)**. Tie a strand of yarn between the circles, hold circles together, and wrap with yarn—the more wraps, the thicker the pom-pom. Cut between the circles and knot the tie strand tightly **(figure 2)**. Place pom-pom between two smaller cardboard circles held together with a needle and trim the edges **(figure 3)**.

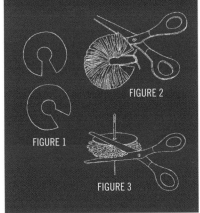

FIGURE 2

FIGURE 1

FIGURE 3

Serpentine COWL
Angela Hahn

Yarnovers create structure rather than lace in the Serpentine Cowl. Patterning is worked every round, creating rapid diagonal movement and revealing the bold motif in relatively little space.

Finished Size

16½" (42 cm) top circumference, 27½" (70 cm) bottom circumference, and 8" (20.5 cm) high.

Yarn

Cascade Yarns Cash Vero (55% merino extrafine wool, 33% microfiber acrylic, 12% cashmere; 98 yd [90 m]/1.75 oz [50 g]): #026 burgundy, 3 skeins.

Needles

Size 8 (5 mm): 20" (51 cm) circular (cir) needle. Adjust needle size if necessary to obtain the correct gauge.

Notions

Markers (m); tapestry needle.

Gauge

19 sts and 25 rows = 4" (10 cm) in St st; 22 sts and 29 rows = 4" (10 cm) in chart patt.

Legend

- ☐ knit
- · purl
- ○ yo
- ╱ k2tog
- ╲ ssk
- ⅄ k3tog
- ⅄ sssk
- ☐ pattern repeat

Serpentine

22 st repeat

Cowl

CO 180 sts. Place marker (pm) and join in the rnd.

RND 1: *K1, p3, k2; rep from * around, pm after every 30th st around (after every 5th patt rep).

RNDS 2–7: Work in rib patt as established.

DEC RND: *K1, ssk, k1, yo, k2, ssk, knit to 9 sts before m, k2tog, k2, yo, k1, k2tog, k1, p1, sl m; rep from * around—12 sts dec'd.

Rep Dec rnd every rnd 3 more times—132 sts rem. Work Rnds 1–20 of Serpentine chart once, then rep Rnds 1–14 once more.

DEC RND 1: *K5, ssk, k2, k2tog, k3, k2tog, k5, p1; rep from * around—114 sts rem.

DEC RND 2: *Ssk, p1, [p2tog] 2 times, k2tog, k1, ssk, p1, p2tog, p1, k2tog, k1; rep from * around—72 sts rem.

NEXT RND: *K1, p3, k2; rep from * around. Rep last rnd 5 more times. BO all sts loosely in patt.

Finishing

Weave in ends. Block to measurements. 🖋

After practicing for many years as a veterinarian, **ANGELA HAHN** decided to practice knitwear design instead. She and her family divide their time between Cape Cod, Massachusetts, and Como, Italy. More can be found on her website, www.knititude.com.

Finished Size
17½ (20)" (44.5 [51] cm) head circumference. Hat shown measures 20" (51 cm).

Yarn
GGH Soft Kid (70% kid mohair, 25% nylon, 5% wool; 150 yd [137 m]/1 oz [25 g]): #075 orange, 1 (2) ball(s). Yarn distributed by Muench Yarns.

Needles
Size 8 (5 mm): 16" (40.5 cm) circular (cir) needle. Size 9 (5.5 mm): 16" (40.5 cm) cir and set of 4 or 5 double-pointed needles (dpn). Adjust needle size if necessary to obtain the correct gauge.

Notions
Marker (m); tapestry needle.

Gauge
16 sts and 24 rows = 4" (10 cm) in zigzag eyelet rib on larger needle with yarn doubled.

Hat

With smaller needle and yarn doubled, CO 70 (80) sts. Place marker (pm) and join in the rnd.

RNDS 1–5: *K3, p2; rep from * to end.

Change to larger needle and work zigzag eyelet rib as foll:

RND 1: *K3, yo, ssk (see Glossary); rep from * to end.

RND 2: *K3, k2tog, yo; rep from * to end.

Rep last 2 rnds until piece measures 5½ (6½)" (14 [16.5] cm) from CO, ending with Rnd 2.

Crown

For size 17½" (44.5 cm), beg with Dec Rnd 3.

DEC RND 1: *K6, k2tog; rep from * to end—70 sts rem for size 20".

RNDS 2, 4, 6, AND 8: Knit.

DEC RND 3: *K5, k2tog; rep from * to end—60 sts rem.

DEC RND 5: *K4, k2tog; rep from * to end—50 sts rem.

DEC RND 7: *K3, k2tog; rep from * to end—40 sts rem.

Size 17½" (44.5 cm) only

DEC RND 9: *K2, k2tog; rep from * to end—30 sts rem.

RND 10: Knit.

Zigzag BEANIE
Dawn Leeseman

Dawn Leeseman uses a mohair blend to subdue but not eclipse the simple zigzagging eyelet pattern of the Zigzag Beanie. With the yarn doubled throughout, a mohair halo gently fills the eyelets and makes the plain sections luxuriously dense.

All sizes

Cut yarn, thread tail onto tapestry needle, draw tail through rem sts twice, pull tight, and fasten off to WS of hat.

Finishing

Weave in loose ends. 🖋

DAWN LEESEMAN lives and teaches knitting classes in Chico, California. She is the co-author of *Casual, Elegant Knits* (Martingale, 2008) with her friend Faina Goberstein.

Easy Peasy SLIPPERS

Lisa Shroyer

Knit these slippers from the cuff to the bottom of the sole. The top of the foot is worked in stockinette with yarnover increases; the bottom is worked in garter stitch.

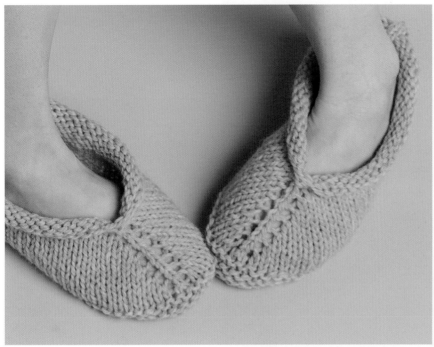

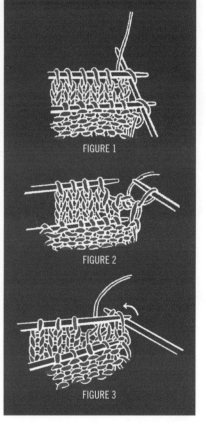

Three-needle bind-off

Place stitches to be joined onto two separate needles. Hold the needles so that right sides of knitting face together. *Insert a third needle into first stitch on each of the other two needles **(figure 1)** and knit them together as 1 stitch **(figure 2)**; knit the next stitch on each needle together in the same way; then pass the firSt stitch over the second **(figure 3)**. Repeat from * until 1 stitch remains on third needle. Cut yarn and pull tail through last stitch.

FIGURE 1

FIGURE 2

FIGURE 3

Finished Size

8½ (10)" (21.5 [25.5] cm) long from back of heel to tip of toe, to fit woman's medium (large); shown in medium size.

Yarn

Cascade Ecological Wool (100% wool; 478 yd [440 m]/9 oz [250 g]): #8016 natural, 1 skein (yarn should be enough for 4 pairs).

Needles

Size 9 (5.5 mm) needles.

Notions

Spare needle for three-needle BO; yarn needle.

Gauge

15 sts and 20 rows = 4" (10 cm) in St st

Slipper (make 2)

CO 47 (59) sts. Knit 1 row.

ROW 1: (RS) K23 (29), yo, k1, yo, k23 (29)—2 sts inc'd.

ROW 2: (WS) Purl.

Rep last 2 rows 7 more times—63 (75) sts.

ROW 3: (RS) Knit.

ROW 4: (WS) Knit.

Rep Rows 3 and 4 four more times.

DEC ROW: (RS) K23 (29), k2tog (see Glossary), k13, k2tog, knit to end—2 sts dec'd.

Knit 1 WS row. Rep last 2 rows 2 more times—57 (69) sts rem. Knit 1 RS row. With WS facing and sts divided into two groups and held parallel on needles, use spare needle to join sts with three-needle BO (see sidebar), working 2 sts tog at toe—no sts rem.

Finishing

Use mattress st (see Glossary) to sew heel seam. Weave in ends. 🍃

LISA SHROYER is the editor of *Knitscene* magazine and the author of *Knitting Plus* (Interweave, 2011).

Finished Size
7½" (19 cm) hand circumference
(stretched) and 7" (18 cm) long.

Yarn
Lorna's Laces Green Line Worsted
(100% organic merino; 210 yd
[191 m]/3.5 oz [100 g]): #501 argyle
(red/blue), 1 skein.

Needles
Size 8 (5 mm) needles.

Notions
4 pins; yarn needle.

Gauge
18 sts and 25 rows = 4" (10 cm) in rib
patt, stretched.

---

stitch guide

K2, P2 Rib (multiple of 4 sts + 2)
Row 1: (RS) K2, *p2, k2; rep from * to
end.
Row 2: (WS) P2, *k2, p2; rep from * to
end.
Rep Rows 1 and 2 for patt.

Mitt (make 2)

CO 34 sts. Work in k2, p2 rib (see
Stitch Guide) for 7" (18 cm). BO all sts
in rib (knitting the knit sts and purling the purl sts as you BO).

Finishing

With one mitt laid flat, place 2 pins
along one side edge as foll: one 1"
(2.5 cm) down from BO edge and
one 2½" (6.5 cm) below the first.
Rep on other edge. Fold mitt in half
lengthwise so that pins at each edge
match up. Use mattress st to sew
seam from CO edge to the lowest
pin. Leave the next 2½" (6.5 cm)
open for thumb opening, then sew
a seam from highest pin to BO edge.
Weave in all ends.

Find out what else **AMY POLCYN** is up
to at www.amypolcyn.com.

Flash MITTS
Amy Polcyn

Make a ribbed rectangle and seam up the sides, while
leaving a thumbhole, and you've got a snug-fitting mitt.
One skein of yarn makes a pair!

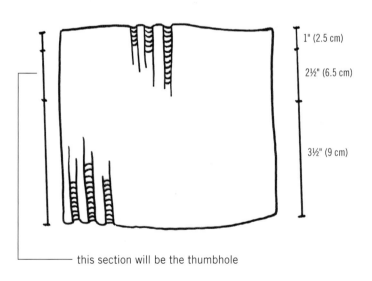

1" (2.5 cm)

2½" (6.5 cm)

3½" (9 cm)

this section will be the thumbhole

Abbreviations

beg	begin(s); beginning		**pwise**	purlwise
bet	between		**RC**	right cross
BO	bind off		**rem**	remain(s); remaining
CC	contrasting color		**rep**	repeat; repeating
cm	centimeter(s)		**rev St st**	reverse stockinette stitch
cn	cable needle		**rib**	ribbing
CO	cast on		**rnd(s)**	round(s)
cont	continue(s); continuing		**RS**	right side
dec(s)	decrease(s); decreasing		**rev sc**	reverse single crochet
dpn	double-pointed needle(s)		**sc**	single crochet
foll	following; follows		**sk**	skip
g	gram(s)		**sl**	slip
inc	increase(s); increasing		**sl st**	slip stitch (sl 1 pwise unless otherwise indicated)
k	knit		**ssk**	slip, slip, knit
k1f&b	knit into front and back of same st		**ssp**	slip, slip, purl
k2tog	knit two stitches together		**st(s)**	stitch(es)
kwise	knitwise		**St st**	stockinette stitch
LC	left cross		**tbl**	through back loop
m(s)	marker(s)		**tog**	together
MC	main color		**WS**	wrong side
mm	millimeter(s)		**wyb**	with yarn in back
M1	make one (increase)		**wyf**	with yarn in front
M1R (L)	make one right (left)		**yo**	yarn over
p	purl		*****	repeat starting point (i.e., repeat from *)
p1f&b	purl into front and back of same st		*** ***	repeat all instructions between asterisks
p2tog	purl two stitches together		**( )**	alternate measurements and/or instructions
patt(s)	pattern(s)		**[ ]**	instructions that are to be worked as a group a specified number of times
pm	place marker			
psso	pass slipped stitch over			
p2sso	pass two slipped stitches over			

Glossary

Backward-Loop Cast-On

*Loop working yarn and place it on needle backward so that it doesn't unwind. Repeat from *.

Crochet Chain (ch)

Make a slipknot on hook. Yarn over hook and draw it through loop of slipknot. Repeat, drawing yarn through the last loop formed.

Crochet Chain Provisional Cast-On

With waste yarn and crochet hook, make a loose crochet chain (see above) about four stitches more than you need to cast on. With knitting needle, working yarn, and beginning two stitches from end of chain, pick up and knit one stitch through the back loop of each crochet chain (**figure 1**) for desired number of stitches. When you're ready to work in the opposite direction, place the exposed loops on a knitting needle as you pull out the crochet chain (**figure 2**).

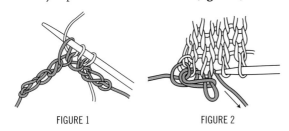

FIGURE 1   FIGURE 2

K2tog Bind-Off

With RS facing, k2tog, *return stitch on right needle to left needle without twisting it, k2tog; rep from *.

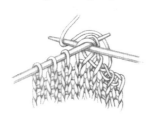

Kitchener Stitch (St st Grafting)

STEP 1: Bring threaded needle through front stitch as if to purl and leave stitch on needle.

STEP 2: Bring threaded needle through back stitch as if to knit and leave stitch on needle.

STEP 3: Bring threaded needle through first front stitch as if to knit and slip this stitch off needle. Bring threaded needle through next front stitch as if to purl and leave stitch on needle.

STEP 4: Bring threaded needle through first back stitch as if to purl (as illustrated), slip this stitch off, bring needle through next back stitch as if to knit, leave this stitch on needle.

Repeat Steps 3 and 4 until no stitches remain on needles.

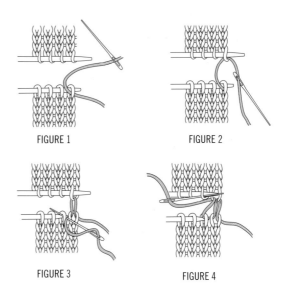

FIGURE 1   FIGURE 2

FIGURE 3   FIGURE 4

Knit 2 Together (k2tog)

Knit two stitches together as if they were a single stitch.

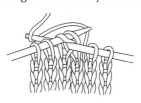

Knitted Cast-On

Place slipknot on left needle if there are no established stitches. *With right needle, knit into firSt stitch (or slipknot) on left needle (**figure 1**) and place new stitch onto left needle (**figure 2**). Repeat from *, always knitting into last stitch made.

FIGURE 1   FIGURE 2

Mattress Stitch Seam

With RS of knitting facing, use threaded needle to pick up one bar between first two stitches on one piece (**figure 1**), then corresponding bar plus the bar above it on other piece (**figure 2**). *Pick up next two bars on first piece, then two bars on other (**figure 3**). Repeat from * to end of seam, finishing by picking up last bar (or pair of bars) at the top of first piece.

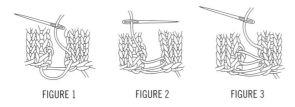

FIGURE 1   FIGURE 2   FIGURE 3

Mattress Stitch for Garter Stitch

STEP 1: Lay the two pieces next to each other, right sides facing up. Thread a tapestry needle with a length of yarn at least three times as long as the area you are sewing.

STEP 2: Working from the bottom up, weave the seaming yarn from front to back on the bottom corner of one piece and then, from back to front, bring it through the bottom corner on the other piece (**figure 1**). Pull the yarn snugly to join the bottom edges.

STEP 3: Insert the needle from bottom to top into the purl bump of a side stitch on one side. Bring the needle up through the bottom edge of the slightly higher stitch on the other piece. Continue sewing on alternate sides in this fashion until you finish the seam (**figure 2**). Pull tightly, and the two pieces should join seamlessly. Weave the yarn end into the seam for a few inches.

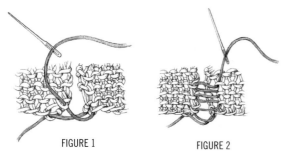

FIGURE 1   FIGURE 2

Purl 2 Together (p2tog)

Purl 2 stitches together as if they were a single stitch.

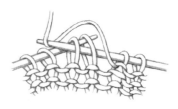

Raised (M1) Increases

Left Slant (M1L) and Standard M1

With left needle tip, lift strand between needles from front to back (**figure 1**). Knit lifted loop through the back (**figure 2**).

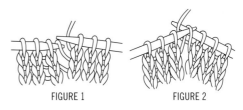

FIGURE 1   FIGURE 2

Right Slant (M1R)

With left needle tip, lift strand between needles from back to front (**figure 1**). Knit lifted loop through the front (**figure 2**).

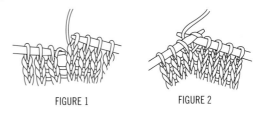

FIGURE 1   FIGURE 2

Purl (M1P)

For purl versions, work as above, purling lifted loop.

Short-Rows (Purl Side)

Work to the turning point, slip the next stitch purlwise to the right needle, bring the yarn to the back of the work (**figure 1**), return the slipped stitch to the left needle, bring the yarn to the front between the needles (**figure 2**), and turn the work so that the knit side is facing—one stitch has been wrapped and the yarn is correctly positioned to knit the next stitch. To hide the wrap on a subsequent purl row, work to the wrapped stitch, use the tip of the right needle to pick up the wrap from the back, place it on the left needle (**figure 3**), then purl it together with the wrapped stitch.

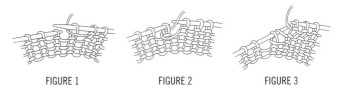

FIGURE 1   FIGURE 2   FIGURE 3

Single crochet (sc)

*Insert hook into the second chain from the hook (or the next stitch), yarn over hook and draw through a loop, yarn over hook (**figure 1**), and draw it through both loops on hook (**figure 2**). Repeat from * for desired number of stitches.

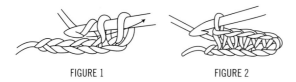

FIGURE 1   FIGURE 2

Slip, Slip, Knit (ssk)

Slip two stitches knitwise one at a time (**figure 1**). Insert point of left needle into front of two slipped stitches and knit them together through back loops with right needle (**figure 2**).

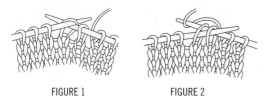

FIGURE 1   FIGURE 2

Standard Bind-Off

Knit the first stitch, *knit the next stitch (two stitches on right needle), insert left needle tip into firSt stitch on right needle (**figure 1**) and lift this stitch up and over the second stitch (**figure 2**) and off the needle (**figure 3**). Repeat from * for the desired number of stitches.

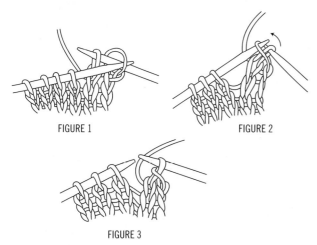

FIGURE 1   FIGURE 2

FIGURE 3

Tubular Cast-On

With contrasting waste yarn, use the backward-loop method to cast on half the desired number of stitches, rounding to the next odd number if necessary (the number can be adjusted after working the cast-on). Cut waste yarn. Continue with working yarn as follows:

ROW 1: K1, *bring yarn to front to form a yarnover, k1 (**figure 1**); repeat from * to end of row.

ROWS 2 AND 4: K1, *bring yarn to front, slip 1 pwise, bring yarn to back, k1 (**figure 2**); repeat from * to end of row.

ROWS 3 AND 5: Bring yarn to front, *slip 1 pwise, bring yarn to back, k1, bring yarn to front; repeat from * to last stitch, slip last stitch.

Continue working k1, p1 rib as desired, removing waste yarn after a few rows.

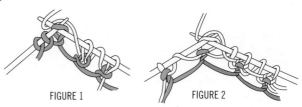

FIGURE 1   FIGURE 2

Find popular patterns for quick and easy projects with these *Craft Tree* publications, brought to you by Interweave.

Crocheted Afghans
ISBN 978-1-62033-094-4

Crocheted Amigurumi
ISBN 978-1-62033-093-7

Crocheted Baby Gifts
ISBN 978-1-59668-739-4

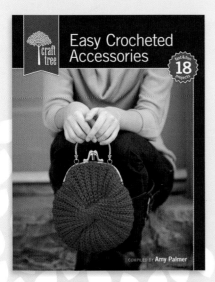

Easy Crocheted Accessories
ISBN 978-1-59668-738-7

Easy Knitted Accessories
ISBN 978-1-62033-092-0

Easy Knitted Hats
ISBN 978-1-62033-097-5

Visit your favorite retailer or order online at interweavestore.com

INTERWEAVE®
interweavestore.com